Night Music

poems by

B. J. Buckley

Finishing Line Press
Georgetown, Kentucky

Night Music

Copyright © 2024 by B. J. Buckley
ISBN 979-8-88838-813-6 First Edition
All rights reserved under International and Pan-American Copyright Conventions. No part of this book may be reproduced in any manner whatsoever without written permission from the publisher, except in the case of brief quotations embodied in critical articles and reviews.

Publisher: Leah Huete de Maines
Editor: Christen Kincaid
Cover Art: "Winter Night" Scratchboard by Dawn Senior-Trask
        Website: fineartamerica.com/profiles/dawnseniortrask
Author Photo: Dainis Hazners
Cover Design: Elizabeth Maines McCleavy

Order online: www.finishinglinepress.com
        also available on amazon.com

        Author inquiries and mail orders:
        Finishing Line Press
        PO Box 1626
        Georgetown, Kentucky 40324
        USA

Contents

I. Hiroshige's Mistress

    Hiroshige's Mistress 1
    Full Moon, Late September 7
    Sumi-e 9
    Aspens 10
    Near Powder River 11
    Three Horses Grazing 14
    Dragonfly 15

II. Playing the Nocturnes

    Playing the Nocturnes, #'s 1—21 19

III. Love and Sorrow (after Neruda)

    Imagine Her 43
    I Dream of Your Body 44
    The Long Grass Weeps Over You 45
    Oh Infinity of Canyons 46
    The Dawn Is Full 47
    So That You Will See Me 48
    Indelible the Way You Stood 49
    Any Part of You 50
    Last Night I Asked the Stars 51
    Come Out of the Rain 52
    How Far Is That Country? 53
    Our Faces Have Disappeared 54

In the Dark 55
Because I Am No Longer Young 56
Worlds End Each Night 57
Dangerous, These Small Hours 58
Do You Think of Me? 59
Little Bat 60
The Raccoons Are Scrabbling 61
The Bowl of the Moon Is Empty 62
Sleepless, I Wander Out 63
The Wind Is Washing the Leaves 64
You Were Lost To Me 65

Acknowledgments 67

Author Biography 69

for Dawn Senior-Trask
poet, artist, lifelong friend

Painting is poetry that is seen rather than felt,
and poetry is painting that is felt rather than seen.
—Leonardo da Vinci

Hiroshige's Mistress

Hiroshige's Mistress: Her Pillow Book

Full moon tonight,
wind.
The blue shadows of pines
sweep the snowy path.
Your footprints,
leading away from me—
nothing can erase them.

Owl.
More melancholy inquiries
in the dark.
What can I say?
I no longer have a name.
The snow is falling again.

*

The moon is drunk on
the sweet wine of my body—
Why, your empty glass?
Every maple, flaming pyre—
if leaves were tears—wind, crying.

*

Open blossoms, rain-
filled, overflowing—scattered
on the damp earth, their
petals, red, each one a flame—

Across my floor, dropped garments.

*

Why drink wine when you
could dip your tongue in this red
blossom, taste sweetness
all night?
    —a little buzzing,
like a bee caught in a rose.

*

The terror of the
body (you said once) watching
hawkfall at twilight
into a meadow too far
to see more than death's shadow.

My Hawk, your descent,
sharp-beaked, into bloody joy—
do you deny it?
My ravished belly, shattered
heart, torn plumage, broken wings

*

Naked in frosted
grass whipped by winds from the south—
oh, sharp cold lashes:
Waiting for fox to come
and lap up the salt of my tears.

*

Remembering you,
I long to recall nothing—
your love bites hot
brands on the flesh of my breasts,
where you rode me, a red ache—

A kiss on the head
erases memory—pine's
icy lips on mine.
I bend to silver tongues of
snow—desiring emptiness.

*

An empty vessel
is already too full—breath,
wind—See? The leaves fall,

unread, the moon's a pale
stain no laundress can remove.

  *

Moonlight tongues my skin
where your rough hands caught me in
their corded snare, held—
marked me. Loosed, my rabbit-heart
pounds, hunter—I dare not move.

  *

That silk dragon who
sleeps in your belly—chain me
to a stone, call him!
 (when he plunges into my
  dark sea, plunges, breathing fire—)

  *

Moon with her bright ropes
binds my wrists, slips silver hands
beneath my slip, pauses—
How long will you sit, shadowed,
to watch her have her way with me?

  *

Rain last night.
There were geese, honking
and calling
above the cloud layer.
At sunrise,
mist rose from the millrace,
wind in the maples—
a thousand
departing wings.

  *

When I see dew
on a red leaf fallen
into the grass, I think—
salt pearls,
fire—
how each curled edge
is a blade.

    *

Yellow soap
in a common shower stall—
the scent of a man I loved,
long ago—
October,
my skin silked with lather—
his hands . . .

    *

My nipples rub
against the rough wool
of my shirt, stand up
hard and red
as the arils of yew.

    *

Between my legs
you were like a horse
drinking after a desperate journey.

So rough, your coarse beard—
I complained—
your thirst was merciless!

Three days ago,
and still I throb and sting.

    *

Yesterday men raked the leaves,
today they are burning them.
Last night I, too, was flame.

*

The moon sank
so slowly
into the cleft
between two mountains—

You entered me—
An eternity, to bend
and string the bow.

*

Spiders have traversed
on silken bridges
our paths between the aspens.
They break across my face—
ghosts of kisses.

*

After moon-set
on our backs in wet grass
we watched meteors
burst across the heavens.

The one that burned hottest
I could not see.

*

You slept—
I moved
from your embrace
to pillow your head
on my open
thighs.

The fragrance
of night-blooming
flowers—
perhaps it will enter
your dream,
awaken you?

        *

I knew that one day
those lessons
on tonguing the flute
to prolong the note
would serve me well.

        *

These verses are for you,
but you have no ear
for poetry.

Perhaps
I should whisper
lines from Wu's treatise
on forging swords?

Full Moon, Late September

What do the colors of autumn say? Not a thing.
Red is not a sound,
nor yellow, orange not the
anguished cry of any bird.

Nor what little green
is left, the death song of frogs
speared by night herons.
Even when it is the ripe
body of sweetness—apple,

maple, plump lips of
a girl—first kiss, or last—red's
profoundly quiet,
stopped heart of a silence so
bone deep it could be water:

Stillness, empty of
all motion, upon which float
rafts of fallen leaves.
Vermilion, scarlet, crimson,
burgundy, rust, carnelian—

it's the busy mind's
voice caressing itself—brick,
maroon, magenta—
the way an infant plays with
its ten tiny toes, enthralled

discovery of
what had been there all along,
wiggling, unnoticed.
As if by our litanies
we could be the wind shaking

the stiff branches of
desire—carmine, ruby, rose—
hectic, flushed, enflamed.
And I could say that blood-rush

which rouges my hot cheeks sings,
or that my fevered swelling, my sanguine
heat, wet fire, is audible—
but it makes no promises,
no vows, whispers no one's name.

Sumi-e

Tonight we will lie down together, pressed body
to body the way leaf presses leaf, waiting
for the moon to rise. All our veins will be visible
through our skin, and because in the darkness
we will be as green as the moon, or as leaves,

no one will see us. The owl will mistake our cries
for light, the paths of our blood for shadows
cast by bare branches. Do not be afraid if,
like the pages of a closed book on the library
shelf, congruent on all surfaces, we cannot

be read, even by each other. Remember
winds and storms and breathing in the folded caves
and hollows of our changeable weather, stories
written in tides and the smell of salt, how lips
leave the intricate impressions of flowers,

red blooms on ivory, an alphabet lost long ago
to voices. Whatever is written in those languages
can still be learned exactly with the fingers.
So it is with us. Our scribbling fades into each
other's skins like a sort of invisible ink.

There is no need to decipher anything. Each letter is
the picture of a sound, a black blossom on rice paper.
Some day a calligrapher will make a brush out of
your soft hair, and paint two dark curves, one
beside the other, almost but not quite touching.

Aspens

What if after all those wings of birds
    had carried them   not
into silence but   too far away
    for us to hear   after
the startled drumming
    of our hearts   had quieted
(who was more
        frightened, we or they?)

it seemed—we were looking,
    looking for them and never saw—

that wind erupted from heartwood
    blasted every leaf into the sky
explosions   screaming   the center
    of the cyclone, *us*   but it was only

a flock of autumn-gathered blackbirds
    taking wing out of the aspens
and perhaps we   had nothing to do with it
at all, were just
              there

when desire unfathomable took hold
and flung them heavenward

what if the   spaces
    where they had been
in the leaves held secret were
                      suddenly
limned by borders of light
    so that we could   see

that luminous
                emptiness
preferable, always
    to hungering   to being filled

Near Powder River

You have hollowed out
my belly the way water
hollows stones—on some
river bottom I am sand
suspended in rushing glass.

I contain nothing,
without being empty, as
summer air holds storm—
everything invisible,
shimmer of heat, clouds and rain.

Stones and red dust, wind.
How like my body, always
thirsty and breathing.
Stones like hills, dust like pollen,
wind flowers—their bold chiming.

All invisible,
the hands, whatever it is
they think they're holding—
my fingers swimming through your flesh
as though we both were air.

This afternoon the
longhorn cattle wandered past,
four calves, the red bull
with his heavy head, roan cow
whose horns had crumpled from the cold.

Sagebrush on dry hills,
ten thousand miniature
trees, soft dusty leaves
whose silver shade is the third
face of rain, wild lark's echo.

Late afternoon sky
is only an empty room
hung with pink curtains,

its walls as transparent as—
ah, you thought I would say air—

but I was thinking
of the transparency of
faces, how always
the skin is like cellophane—
its wrinkles refract the light.

I wish we were the
moon, so that we could have four
bodies, two slender,
two full—scimitar, snake in
water, womb or well, bonfire.

Too dry for April—
some eager spark leaped towards the
white arms of the grass—
when it's done, there's nothing left
of either of us but smoke.

All day the burning
irrigation ditches sent
up harsh blue incense—
last year's cattails, carcasses
of deer who met death running.

Where Piney Creek slows
and curves, herons ride the masts
of old cottonwoods,
grey-blue wings stretched wide like sails
to catch one last breath of light.

A lone kingfisher
sits jade still, statue quiet,
on an electric
wire near the railroad tracks, soft
prayer of green waiting.

The new moon bestows
darkness like a gift—showers
of meteors burn
fiery signatures across
the dusky breasts of evening.

Orion hungers
in the western sky for his
she-bear gone hunting
over the edge of the world—
taut bright bow, empty arrows.

At the far borders
of this country of lantern
light, bats sing circles
of wing and hunger, owls drift
like clouds in the outer dark.

If I am earth and you are water,
you will wash me away.

If I am earth and you are air,
you will move over me while I sleep
and I will not awaken.

If I am earth and you are fire,
will you be the sun or the full moon,
will I be ice, or ashes?

If I am earth and you are earth,
silence will cover us,
we will cover each other,
wild stars will cover heaven.

Let us say that lips
open and close like red wings
while rivers unhindered
flow beneath the tenuous
bridges of our bright breathing.

Three Horses Grazing

Detail, Chinese Silk Screen, Yuan Dynasty,
Thirteenth Century, by an Anonymous Painter

Seven hundred years of grass, pale yellow, straw yellow
(it must be autumn) stretch so far into the sky that the horizon
is mute. There is no edge to the field, no last fence
or stone post, no natural barrier cast up of hills
or far mountains, no cloudy heaven mimicking landscape,

only clouds of pollen veiling the horses like a mist.
One is eating, the roan; and next to him, a black mare
with white blazing her face like last light illuminating sheer cliffs
has her head askew on her neck and her ears laid back—is
the contest for one choice tuft worth nips and tussle

when she has abundance at her own feet and the day is fading?
Perhaps. The eyes of both horses are lanterns in fog, gold and golden.
Butt into the wind and his tail whipping out a single brushstroke
against the papery air, a third horse faces the invisible border
of meadow and waits for the girl child to bring him hard yellow pears,

first bloom of chrysanthemum from her window box, sugar!
He knows she is coming and he is patient in his hunger. The bickering
of his companions, the diminished light, cool wind growing sharper
into evening, nothing can touch the absolute sure joy of his anticipation.
His bones are dust, that man who painted this buckskin horse,

this shadow on translucent silk whose skin still quivers with desire
for the touch of a small white hand on his neck,
bursts of sweetness on his tongue.

Dragonfly

it hung
shimmering in the horsetail
reeds   tiny monster
     its church window wings

poised   still   and
myself on tiptoe   stealthy
through the watergrass   I wanted
     to get closer

to be magnified
to be   alone   a multitude reflected
in the fun-house mirrors
     of its eyes

before it rattled out
over the water   at last   I bent
took it into my hand   unmoving
brilliant jewel

banked fire in the glimmering
grass and perfect   all
unbroken   the wire legs   the glass
     wings   the globed blind

eyes   and it weighed
nothing   was so
heavy   this mysterious
     dying   as if

its soul and
body had lit   together
and one was startled into quick
     flight by my

shadow or the sound
of my held breath
into the ecstasy of leaving
     even that small shell
behind

Playing the Nocturnes

Playing the Nocturnes

#1 in *B-flat minor*

Night falls fast.
Storm swept light
with a broom of snow,
pale, crystalline,
so fine it hangs in the howling air
like veils.

Night,
throat filled with voices:
pine branch
bent by whiteness,
blizzard-blinded deer.
The wind, its indecipherable
languages,
stars,
their flames blown out.

#2 in *E-flat major*

Moon.
Only One—
Imagine the thin membranes
of our skin dissolved,
our muscles parted, our veins
opened
to radiance.

Light can be both wave and particle.

Our hearts,
their lunar certainty,
towards,
away from—

one breath, one
small pause

changes everything.

#3 in *B major*

It was so dark, so dark, the water
thick with cold
enough to slow
the current, we were moving
so steadily we felt
still,
and it was the world
in two dark boats on either side of us
that was vanishing.

There are pages missing.

We'll never know.

#4 in *F major*

When someone kisses
the moist air
above the cheek of a sleeping
child,
and she stirs—
breath,
that slightest

faltering

remember
how the river at spring runoff
sang to you, to you,
how you knew
if you had been older,
or ill,
or sadder,
you'd have leapt into its music
unafraid

#5 in *F-sharp major*

The birds, so quiet all day
in the deep cold
break their hunger—
last gathering—
sparrows,
finches,
nuthatches in pairs
mining crevices
of bark.
And ravens, the black uncles, sorrowing
in the stripped carcass
of a deer.
Red-tail hawk. A stillness
with wings.

#6 in *G minor*

At twilight, the owls'
assertive questioning—
from the pine near the cabin, one call
immense and pitched low,
a cello;
from the aspens an adolescent,
cocky, but undone
by a voice that cracks suddenly
into the upper registers:
squeaky, out-of-tune
clarinet. Undaunted
clarinet. It goes on and on and
on, all night, this dozens game
high in the snowy trees,
this awkward uneven pleading
of desire.
The female's somewhere, listening.
She could be in the next county
and she'd still hear them!
Choose, sweet one.
All of us could use a juicy mouse
and some sleep.

#7 in *C-sharp minor*

Wakefulness.
Fragile voles throbbing in the grass, twitch
of tiny whiskers,
soft churr of nested birds
who've mistaken the moon
for morning.

Little bats harvest the fields of the air.

Fox, hunting, coyote, hunting, the neighbor's
lop-eared cat, slaughterer
of deer mice,
cowled deer cloistered in the
aspens.

Oh, the silk of darkness
falling, falling away,
skin-silk, tongue-silk, all the quick
devouring—
so close: in the meadow,
in the pines,
along the narrow ditch, in the clear
water.

The owls
have finished their fierce
copulations,
there's an ache in their bellies
they'll mistake for hunger.

#8 in *D-flat major*

Between the bird—its azure wing—
and the quick blue
in the eye—unbridgeable
distance.

Impossible to keep—
brief echo of this world.
The space we sought the bird in, empty,
its sweet note vanished.

Your lips brush away
before I can feel
your kiss.

#9 in *B major*

Rain after months of drought,
the leaves—
scrub maple, water birch, black poplar,
willow.
Tamarack—her yellow needles fall.

Brief hollows where woodpeckers fledged,
where the owls nested,
where violet-green swallows came and went
through tiny doors.

Cast yourself upon the single mercy
of this world: Nothing
endures. Nothing
lasts.
Silence, that good dog, follows.
Each shift
like the dough of good bread
being turned
and turned and
left in the dark
to rise.

#10 in *A-flat major*

We close our eyes, we turn
away, no fear
or grief, without
a touch
a kiss
a thought
a breath

How is it that nothing
                       holds us?

#11 in *G minor*

Is the plainchant of owls
indelible?

Do little birds waking with song to moonlight
dye the stars yellow? Or red? Or blue?

The hard white paper of your bones—
silent bats have scribbled there.

Owls spill rondels of longing.

The grave's cold stones have mouths,
and sing

#12 in *G major*

The parable's partly right:
the last will be first, if only
into the grave.
Treasure is of this world, no other—
crown or coin,
cadenced melodies of wind
in taut-strung pines—
no need, after all, for clavichord
or pianoforte,
those instruments inferior
to goose cry, chortling owls,
snow mixed with rain flung chill
against the grass—

Don't hurry.
Drag your feet.
Lie down in the meadow, or
like the man fallen among thieves,
by the highwayside.
There's Venus.
Fragile crescent of new moon.
Damp earth.
The red or yellow willow.

Passersby will fling alms at you,
thinking you a beggar,
and drunk besides.
Be drunk, then,
on this precipitous edge
of spring, on wine
or merely breathing, be
a beggar:
coin or curse, say
Yes. Say
That's my heart's desire.

#13 in *C minor*

Paper. Ink. Straight
lines, small circles filled in black
or hollowed out, dots
and curlicues and signs,
sound or silence, speed
or
hesitation, yes or
no—
a broken thread.
An unstringing
of small dark pearls.

#14 in *F-sharp minor*

Who would want to live
forever?   It's nearly morning.
The moon is low in the sky, the stars
can hardly stay awake—
one by one their cold eyes
close.
Lay me down
in the grass, undress
my heart—
the empty sky presses down
like a kiss. Delicate ants explore
my hair, my breasts
are soft moons.
Tiny beetles come to me
as if I had spoken:
at the end, my flesh—
its language
of dark perfumes—
and they'll attend me.
Who could want to say no
to them? Whose dust could refuse
the wild hand of the wind,
its voice begging   *Let me,*
                                      let me

#15 in *F minor*

The sky gets lost,
wanders off, follows
some errant crow
on its black journey.
The pines
stretch up to fill the void
with green
darkness,
their backs curved by wind
walking over them,
until above us
all is pine,
stars impaled
on every needle,
uncountable.
Snow falls.
Now, in the hush,
and now, and
now—
one pine needle crushed
between the teeth,
sharp sweet green
knife
to the heart.

#16 in *E-flat major*

What separates this world
from the next one
is so nearly part of us
that we've already crossed over
and back again a thousand times,
carrying tired invisible children
whose eyelids drift shut,
closing the doors
of light.
And soon the little phantoms
are asleep,
their heads rested
on our shoulders, soft weight
we will always carry.

#17 in *B major*

Night music—
dark
itself, the songs
of shadow.
We grow up without knowing
that we're wax, lit candles
in a cold room
of stars.

It's early March, and the great owls
have nested—
uneven clutch of eggs,
hard throbbing planets—
within them,
little earthquakes
of down and talon,
tremors, aftershocks of
whatever shock the wild bloody love
of owls must be.

This soft tearing we do
at each other's flesh—
perhaps we were owls, once,
or scarlet fox-flame,
strewing quick small pools of gladness
across cornfields buried
in early snow.

#18 in *E major*

Intricate tangle,
all unwoven—
silk into salt,
satin to iron, muddy wool,
pollen and petal
that once were gossamer.
Perfect orb
of perfect spider,
the moon in pale damask,
stars stitched
to the dark—sequined velvet,
in another life:
a waistcoat,
a soft bodice?
Let the fingers of this music
fumble
all your tiny
buttons,
allow its little hands
to unlace your shoes.

Answer, Tailor: *What's
this melody?*
    Cloth of skin
    on a loom of bone.
Who's the weaver?
    No One.
    Anyone.
    Each thread, our long
    unraveling.

#19 in *E minor*

By the time we finally learn,
it's too late: the clock of the body
turns over the hours,
the days,
our faces, like pages in a book—
half-glimpsed, half-known,
gone.
The clock of the heart has odd hitches
in its ticking, missed beats,
and between them,
timeless—
our fingers, fragile deer running
through forests of soft hair,
that glance over a shoulder,
fragments of song—
and then the drum keeps drumming, then
the march over the edge.
And we're always
leaping,
the sonata half-memorized,
our fingers, old or young, so clumsy
with desire—grass, pear, belly,
pine,
we're too small
to hold it.
We do what caught animals do—
we press against the walls
and they give way:
this life, no body can contain
or outlast it,
and who knows
if stars know what love is
or if God remembers anything
beyond that first loneliness,
that first division between water
and light.

#20 in *C-sharp minor*

> "... for where your treasure is,
> there shall your heart be also..."

Here, then.
Shattered birds decay
beneath decaying leaves,
their eggs abandoned to the appetites
of skunks and foxes.
Leaves fall, and then the snow,
and then the winter living
in our bones.
Oh, beauty, when the hail
tears green needles from the pines
and wheat three days from harvest
lies beaten flat into the muddy fields.
I do know
what I am choosing:
age and loss
and death and all desires broken
on the altar of unbearable
sweetness:
Rain perfumes the grass.
Listen—that dark
silence just before
coyotes court the moon.

#21 in *C minor, Posthumous*

Forget I ever was.
The cough, the piano, feverish hands
scribbling notes across the pages.
Music passed through me
like a ghost through empty rooms.
The melodies burning.
A fire not yet gone cold.

Love and Sorrow
after Neruda

Imagine Her

Imagine her, fifty. The girl
she was, alive in her body,
a body that has not forgotten itself.

Imagine the knock at the door,
courier on the step, a packet of pages
tied with red ribbon.

How she takes it, her fingers fumbling
the knot, the ribbon frayed,
its color the color of blood, maple leaves, ripe apples.

Watch—she unfolds
each brittle sheet, the paper yellowed,
fading ink, his words

as she reads them, embers
blown to flame.

The years are too heavy.
The years fall away—

they're nothing.

I Dream Of Your Body

I dream of your body, a man's body, landscape
underpinned with bone, my country of rivers,

horse rearing to cover a mare, tree
thrust for water into the red well of my belly.

I was solitary under the dark pines. Their boughs
were the walls of a room where owls were

my Inquisitors. Night drowned me. To live,
I pressed my lips to yours, breath of wind

that in autumn scatters the leaves from the poplars.
I became that angel who offers her yellow pages

to those who cannot remember letters. I loved you,
though my heart became one of the stones of your mountain.

Carnal moonlight, torso with hillocks of dark
curled grass. Oh, the teeth you have stolen

from tigers! Sweet milk that my tongue
teased out, a nectar of honey and bitter and salt!

How formidable, your body which is as hard
as absence. My belly, shipwrecked,

the tides of your longing flowing over the hull,
your wind that tatters the sails of my long hair.

You have put out my only compass, the cold stars.

The Long Grass Weeps Over You

The long grass weeps over you tears of green flame.
How could you not be empty? Wind has taken their seed

and in the twilight, wraiths of the meadow
approach you like shy antelope.

I have no more words. My darling,
it is an awful truth, how much we love

our loneliness, how friendly we are
with Death, brilliant sun hanging in ruins around us.

There are two eggs concealed in the soft cloth
of your pocket. Out of your heart some Darkness

arises, a giantess putting on her purple dress
to welcome the deer and the comets, who are

hiding from us, though they were born from our
congresses, though we always offer them bread and apples.

Oh, beloved captive of the spinning
carousel of stars, from crimson to dark ocher

autumn dyes your garments—wake up, awaken me!—
our last flowers are blackening with frost, full of a delicate despair.

Oh Infinity Of Canyons

Oh infinity of canyons, whisper of eons
walking tiptoe over the pines, moonlight, owl chiming

alone, water falling behind your eyes, little bear,
meadow, out of whom echoes the green song of amorous crickets!

In you thunder howls, and the wolf in me
answers your voracity; like a wild dog you set me to coursing the deer.

Draw me like a bow and in the madness of my submission
you arrows will fly sharper than the beaks of eagles.

I am in you, as if your body were a mist
caressing the fur between my thighs, ghost

tormenting me with cold wet hands. Kiss me there,
I am red as hibiscus pearled with rain.

Because you speak in a forgotten language,
your voice is an impenetrable mystery,

belling like a tiny wren from the bushes of evening;
the wheat is ripe, and the corn,
the crows offer you their black kisses.

The Dawn Is Full

The dawn is full of dust
at the broken edge of October.

Beautiful clouds bid farewells of pink sugar,
riding piggy-back on the moon's broad shoulders.

No one can count the metered hearts of air—
they are as numberless as our unspoken caresses.

God, tired of being in charge, is playing his old violin
at our table, our loins are at war among the plates.

Hurricane, gale, icy warrior lopping off the heads
of chrysanthemums, cyclone with its hand on the breasts of birds—

I want to be the wind that breaks you like ancient pine,
so you fall, your whole weight, into my consuming fires,

your kisses like brands, your body lightning,
bright door, the gathering storm.

So That You Will See Me

So that you will see me
my rhymes sometimes shed their skins,
become shadows on warm stone.

Adornment, tiny cymbals
for your thighs, juicier than plums.

I watch the skeletons of my verses from so far away
that they forget me to follow you.
They become stray dogs, begging for scraps.

At night they sleep on your porch,
they twitch in their dreams of you—

it is all your fault that the silk of my hair
does not cover them, that they have fallen
out of my mouth.

When I did not know you, they crept up onto my couches.
I grew used to their slumbering heads heavy on my breasts.

I want to teach them to speak on command to you,
I want you to understand
the lolling red tongues of their language.

Leashes clipped to their collars tug them away.
The scent storms under bushes excite them to ecstasy.

When they sniff at the crotches of passers by,
that's me, in disguise, oh, sorrow, not you,
not you, the worn jeans

of strangers, their empty pockets. Come back,
come back as though you had always intended to,
with a stick for a gift, a green ball, a bone.

Indelible The Way You Stood

Indelible the way you stood
on the threshold between disturbances and seasons,

you, a ragged shirt, a sparrow's stillness.
Shy ferns sprouted among the stones of your singing.

Entwined with me, as a small stream
braids gravel into its liquid body, we

were so silent, a church of quietness
with flaming altars, my soul burning in your gift of sleep.

Fragrant trout lily, the fins of your petals
are spotted with the blood of summer—winter is a dream

we haven't dreamed yet. Shirt full of holes,
quick weasel hunting in the needle duff,

little sharp teeth of your wanting.
Early mist hung above the cold river,

I cannot forget you, your bones made of burnt apple trees.
Beyond your voice frogs spill their jelly into muddy pools.

Any Part Of You

Any part of you would be enough, enough for me—
the softness of your hair scattered across my pillow.

Or if you were deeply sleeping, your small nipples,
which my fingers could find, little mushrooms in the moss—

your chest, its planes and angles blurring, how breath
is a persistent wind that erodes the open prairie of the flesh,

carrying it invisibly away. Or—if you were dreaming,
unable to prevent me, I could lay my hand

on your belly to feel in it the rise and fall, slow swell
of tides, how the moon pulls and pulls—or lower, the cup

of my palm, so gently, fondling the unhatched eggs
of your desire, so gently, not waking them—only to hold

them in a warm nest—shell of hope, fluttering of tiny feathers,
imagined song, pulse that will one morning stretch out a wing.

Last Night I Asked The Stars

Last night I asked the stars to write you a letter
in their bright script, in the legible hand of light,
surely you will be able to read it?

I have sent you urgent messages on the winter telegraph
of bare twig and branch, tap-tap, tap-tap, the wind's cold fingers
echoing the hesitant dots, the dashes of blackbirds.

With pencils of blood, with pencils of tears, I have scribbled
the letters of my name on the autumn leaves,

they are being mailed to you, the letters of my name
which you once traced elegantly in your notebooks.

I have dialed the circle of seasons, every number
in the phone books of summer which might be yours—

the little warblers are ringing, ringing
in the tops of cottonwoods, please answer?

This morning I wrapped up my heart's paper, bent corners,
all of the exclamations jotted down in its margins, its fading type,
I wrapped it up like a small fish in a newspaper tied with white string,

I will give it to the first stranger I meet, you must ask
everyone, what is it they have, that small parcel in a coat pocket?

Come Out Of The Rain

Come out of the rain, its grey needles
stitching the pines to the side of the mountain,
maples scattering tears of red paper.

The moon presses her blue thumb to my forehead,
then waves goodbye. Dark parabolas
pierce the dusty rings of Saturn.

Little boy that you were, sometimes your shadow
crosses the welling of clouds like an expression of grief.

Tumult of your limbs, a song so furious
you pass like a bird who forgets all that is not sky.
The breath of autumn, withering us.

Great pines are uprooted and fallen.
You, slender boy, horsetail reed, legs of the heron—
you were the reason aspens gave alms to the wind,

you, pale snow, corn stubble,
you, who erased all the pages of my voice.

How Far Is That Country?

How far is that country where I could talk with you
again, as if I were a young girl? So far, that place

in which I could stand before you in my skin,
as uncurtained as a window.

Here are the things I am no longer allowed to speak of—
because yes, I will say it, soon I will be that old woman

whose ample buttocks move under her skirt
like a sack full of puppies.

These things—how my lips grow swollen
from tonguing your name, how I dream the strong smell
of your loins, sweet reek so pungent

after a day of working that it permeates your clothes,
and my dress is not the only thing that grows wet,
when I kneel down to the laundry—

how inside the soft house of my belly
there are sweet rooms you have never lived in,

where I would make you a bed, where I would be
the liquid fire of poppies whose petals, forever,
are as young as the moon.

Our Faces Have Disappeared

Our faces have disappeared into the fading river.
There was no witness to the kisses we scattered
for the ducks, while darkness shook out her blue tablecloth.

Once from my cabin door I watched the aurora,
incendiary dresses sparking through the pines.

Another time the moon dropped dust in my emptiest pockets,
and I spent it on weapons and scars.

Why couldn't I find you?
Who held you? What secrets?

How is it that love pours down like rain
when I am full of sorrow and you are busy vanishing?

The book I read in your absence has erased its pages,
and my sheets are pitifully dragging their broken wings.

You are always falling away at evening
towards that place where the dark goes
unweaving our cities.

In The Dark

In the dark that lives inside the hours of morning,
closeted with the small bodies of owlets, with fragrances

of muskrat and weasel, I am lighting the bright lamp
of forgetting, I am learning to remember.

Because I drank the water of kisses from your mouth,
water both frigid and on fire, my blood is no longer

my blood only, but a liquid echo of the red rush
swirling through you, somewhere—and the same

is true of you, that my heart's skipped beats cause
your own to leap, to buzz its bee wings, to slow

at times like this, when the sun is blacker than mink
or otter hunting along the slough before dawn.

Because I Am No Longer Young

Because I am no longer young, because my breasts
sag, their heaviness resting in your palms—

my urgent ardor, my hunger in old clothes.
Lie down with me in the arms of autumn! Your shirt of leaves,

your face turned to the sky, full of rain.
Listen, listen, the wild geese are crying

in my hair, entangled with winter cloud, my face
is a map in soft clay of that desert country

where I wandered in search of you. In the arroyos—
we are still hiding there! I am your velvet bed of lichens,

shorn wool smelling of ewe's milk and sage. Oh, in your sleeves
of red maple lie down in my arms, in this dead world, for love.

Worlds End Each Night

Worlds end each night, whole worlds disappear
as though they had never been—the moon, her slow fall

behind the mountain, the stars, little fireflies, surrendering
their lanterns to the dawn. Voices—chirr of crickets,

amorous frog-song, little bats, the whistle of their hunger
fluting through the dark, the owl's interrogations of

the infinite—all silenced, all quieted. And you,

whose orbit all my longings trace, my longings, a hundred moons
spinning a luminous cloth around that emptiness

that was once a dark cup filled with you—how I drank!—
in what convolutions of the vastness are you dancing,

behind what veils of the dust of the stars? My heart's a telescope
scanning the darkest reaches—you were so large,

so bright, oceans and continents, poles of ice and fire—
your storms, now, so invisible, your calms, so silent.

Dangerous, These Small Hours

Dangerous, these small hours, when the night is no longer
night, when morning is not yet the morning.

Tiny bats, their hunger sated, fly purely for joy,
ash floats on the wind from all the bodies burning.

Small birds go quiet in their nests, they damp down
their heartbeats to survive the chill.

The aspens stand slender as the limbs of a girl,
white statues in the moonlight.

Mice cease their scrabbling in the grass.
The vixen pricks up her ears.

Somewhere, a cry,
blood-scent, quick snap of teeth—

Slumber cradles you, in your narrow bed, in the back of the house,
in a quiet neighborhood, in a small city,

and the maples press their red palms to the window
as if they might kiss the cool glass of your face—

I could stand there, watching you,
you wouldn't know me—

you'd think thief, think she-bear in her nightgown of dark
fur come to rob oil seed from your pretty finches—

You wouldn't dream of a young girl
prisoned in the flesh of a woman,

her desire a white flame curled
softly against the contours of your body as you sleep.

Do You Think Of Me?

Do you think of me, when you are walking somewhere
along a sidewalk, in shoes with thin soles? When a bird

in its shadowy dress clatters up towards the air, little ship
of feathers, little sails of its wings, towards the sky, do you remember

oceans, how I was the tide, how you were the moon?
I think perhaps your heart has amnesia, though in every city I search

the sad pages of phone books for your name—sad phone books,
all of those numbers unloved by anyone. Some nights I've

dialed them, the secret codes of strangers, pretending—
The park? I say, the Japanese lanterns?

Feeding bread to the gulls on the beach in a gale? We were
young, you've forgotten, but I cannot forget you

in your worn Levis torn out at the knee. There must be a girl
who kept their photographs, fair girls who lost their area codes,

do you think of me,
not knowing it's me you're recalling,

when the phone rings, and someone hangs up before you can say
Hello?

Little Bat

Little bat, little drunkard, inebriate
of evening, impulse and echo, your flight!

Oh shuttle, small weaver of fabrics of hunger,
I feel your voice—exquisite tremble—my walls

of skin, that long to release you, moth of my heart
that awaits your devouring!

Skin-winged, furred, heat-seeking missile
launched at the carapace of midnight,

your bead-bright eyes, cured of blindness!
Velvet coat, kidskin, petals of rose!

Little bat, whose song I am deaf to!

Here in my hand, sweet thumb of your body,
in your belly two eggs of the moon are asleep.

Here is the darkness, your famished measure—
Here, the soft raindrops, the stray mosquitoes!

All the stars are undressed, the stars stand naked.
From the long grasses the fireflies flicker their saddest lanterns.

Little bat, absent, vanished from evening,
your wings still alive in the pages of hours.

Little bat, whose song I am deaf to!

The Raccoons Are Scrabbling

The raccoons are scrabbling in the furrows between corn rows,
ring-tails, their hands small and dexterous—into their cheeky pockets,

the desiccated kernels of summer's corn, little tiles whose letters
spell yellow, whose letters spell sleek and fat.

I am holding your hand, disguised as the wind's hand, your hand
in a glove of sere leaf, dried stalk, the bones of your hand

in their masks of small stones which I found in a wet clod of earth.
I am entwining my fingers with yours, how thin your fingers,

stalks of shorn wheat, or barley, so thin.
The milkweed pods bursting—your hair, gone white,

gone weightless, like foam on the little crests of waves,
your hair, moonlight, which I kissed once, which I kiss.

The Bowl Of The Moon Is Empty

The bowl of the moon is empty
as the hollow of a tree in autumn

after the woodpeckers who nested there
have fledged and flown. The stars

are small pinholes in dark paper,
the nothing that shines through

is so bright. My feet are wet
from walking in the meadow,

the hem of my nightgown
soaked with dew. The moon

is an empty bowl. I remember
lying down inside her curve with you,

I remember us falling and burning out
like meteors.

Sleepless, I Wander Out

Sleepless I wander out into the moon's hallway,
a silver corridor with many doors, all shut, all quiet.

Behind one of them, perhaps, you too are pacing
in a small chamber, trailing the smoke of a dream

behind you. In each of your footsteps starlight
pools on the carpet, its design and patterns

curling like vines around your ankles, their tendrils
kissing your ankles, trying to hold you—

I could tell them that you are a green horse, wilder
than any horse that has ever lived, that no one,

not even I, could catch, or keep.

The Wind Is Washing The Leaves

The wind is washing the leaves and hanging them to dry
on the slenderest twigs, the thinnest branches, the wind

is laundering the old clothes worn by willow and cottonwood,
so ragged, so yellow, torn and spattered insect wing, burned

by early frosts. If I had a shirt, one shirt you had worn
until your elbows poked through like the scrawny wings

of a fledgling heron, a shirt with a frayed collar, a small
stain, loose button hanging by a blue thread like a tiny

moon suspended from a pocket, I could let the wind
take it up in her hands, I could let the air's clean body

pretend, for awhile, that it loved me, though we both
were so poor, and dressed in rags.

You Were Lost To Me

You were lost to me the first time I opened—flower,
door—What shall I do with the corners of air?

They shimmer like ghosts of your graceful body.
I was the horse you tamed with oats and apples,

I was the wild horse you broke to your will,
harsh bit in my mouth, spurs in my haunches.

Bright wind of your breath, swallowed by sky,
how shall I lure it away from the clouds,

back again into the cage of your ribs,
when you leave the door to it always open?

When we are dust, how will I know which swirling grains
were the soil of you, rich loam, generous field

of your embraces? Salt of the sea, tides of heartbeat,
blood's estuaries, where? Because you have vanished

I take off my skirts, press my body to stones—
There is your heat! My Sun, locked in granite!

Or the spent coolness of your skin, moonlight—
there, there—but you've slipped out

and into the dress of deer, into a coat of dark pines.
Your footprints disappear into thickets of willow,

the branches of willow, yellow and red and thin and bare,
bluest shadows, how quiet is this winter country of your absence.

Little shells, remember! Your ears that I kissed, pink
labyrinths, my lost voice wandering there, my whispers—

Stones, do not forget! Bone's architecture, frame
of the hollow of your palm beneath a breast, snake curve

of your spine in sleep. The skin of pale ice on the pond this morning,
your skin that was ivory and alabaster!

No matter how desperately I exhort the roses
to bloom, to flame up—your lips, your cheeks—
they have stopped paying attention to me. Their petals fall,
they fall, they consort in silence with shattered maple.

How is it that you have melted like early snow?
I would sew up my heart with a thread

of crows, I would mend the worn shoes
of my despair. Oh, beyond starlight, farther than far—

Even the wild geese betray me with their longing!
Aligned to their invisible compass, wild geese calling in darkness.

Acknowledgments

Briar Cliff Review, The wind is washing the leaves

Comstock Review, Last night I asked the stars; Because I am no longer young; How far is that country?

december, Dangerous, these small hours; Come out of the rain

Green Mountains Review, Little bats; The raccoons are scrabbling; Full Moon, Late September

Hole in the Head Review, Three Horses Grazing

Lummox Anthology 2019, Do you think of me?; You were lost to me

Lummox Contest Winner, Hiroshige's Mistress, Her Pillow Book

Pilgrimage, Playing the Nocturnes #14, #16, #19, #20, and #21

Sky Island Journal, So that you will see me; Indelible, the way you stood

Spinoza Blue, Sleepless, I wander out; The bowl of the moon is empty; Our faces have disappeared

Surface Design, Volume 19, No. 3: Playing the Nocturnes, #18 in E Major, in slightly different form as, Chopin: The Nocturnes, #18 in E Major Opus 62 No. 2: Lento

The Missoulian, Dragonfly

Inspiration for the poems in *Night Music* came from several sources; suggested links are included below for those with a further interest:

Long years of viewing the glorious woodcuts of Hiroshige in books, museums, and online.   https://en.wikipedia.org/wiki/Hiroshige

Since my first childhood piano lessons, playing myself and listening to—on vinyl, cassette, CD, in live performance, and online—Chopin's Nocturnes, by as many different pianists as possible.

I spent a whole year re-learning to play them while writing the middle section of this book.
https://en.wikipedia.org/wiki/Nocturnes_(Chopin)
19 of the Nocturnes performed by Arthur Rubinstein
https://www.youtube.com/watch?v=wuL7UC2glJM

Reading and re-reading, in both Spanish and English, since my teens, Pablo Neruda's *Twenty Love Poems and a Song of Despair,* published when he was only 19. https://en.wikipedia.org/wiki/Twenty_Love_Poems_and_a_Song_of_Despair

Rural Montana poet and writer **B. J. Buckley** has taught in Arts-in-Schools and Communities programs throughout the West and Midwest for nearly five decades. She has conducted residencies on Native American Reservations, in refugee resettlement centers, museums, libraries, senior and dementia care centers, homeless shelters, and healthcare facilities. She was for several years the Writer-in-Residence at Sanford Cancer Center in Sioux Falls, SD.

Her prizes and awards include a Wyoming Arts Council Literature Fellowship and a Montana Arts Council ARPA Grant; *The Cumberland Poetry Review*'s Robert Penn Warren Narrative Poetry Prize; *Poets & Writers* "Writers Exchange Award" in Poetry; the Rita Dove Poetry Prize from the Center for Women Writers at Salem College, Winston-Salem, NC; the Joy Harjo Prize from CutThroat, A Journal of the Arts; *the Comstock Review* Poetry Prize; and Honorable Mention in *Southern Humanities Review*'s Witness Prize. She has been awarded residencies at The Ucross Foundation, the Vermont Studio Center, and the Colrain Manuscript Conference.

B. J.'s books include *Artifacts*, Willow Bee Press; *Moon Horses and the Red Bull*, ProngHorn Press, with co-author Dawn Senior-Trask; and *Corvidae: Poems of Ravens, Crows, and Magpies*, Lummox Press. Her chapbook manuscript, *In January, the Geese*, won the Comstock Review's 35th Anniversary 2021 Poetry Chapbook Prize. *Flyover Country*, Pine Row Press, was published in June 2024.

You can find her recent work in *About Place Journal, Grub Street, Dogwood, Calyx, Hole in the Head Review, Oakwood, Willow Springs*, and many other print and online magazines.

www.ingramcontent.com/pod-product-compliance
Lightning Source LLC
Chambersburg PA
CBHW020340170426
43200CB00006B/448